# How to use this book

*Follow the advice, in italics, given for you on each page.*
*Support the children as they read the text that is shaded in cream.*
***Praise*** *the children at every step!*

*Detailed guidance is provided in the Read Write Inc. Phonics Handbook*

## 9 reading activities

*Children:*
*Practise reading the speed sounds.*
*Read the green, red and challenge words for the story.*
*Listen as you read the introduction.*
*Discuss the vocabulary check with you.*
*Read the story.*
*Re-read the story and discuss the 'questions to talk about'.*
*Read the story with fluency and expression.*
*Answer the questions to 'read and answer'.*
*Practise reading the speed words.*

# Speed sounds

## Consonants  *Say the pure sounds (do not add 'uh').*

| f<br>ff<br>(ph) | l<br>ll<br>le | m<br>mm | n<br>nn<br>(kn) | r<br>rr | s<br>ss<br>se | v<br>ve | z<br>zz | sh | th | ng<br>nk |
|---|---|---|---|---|---|---|---|---|---|---|
| b<br>bb | c<br>k<br>ck | d<br>dd | g<br>gg | h | j | p<br>pp | (qu) | t<br>tt | w<br>(wh) | x | y | ch<br>tch |

## Vowels  *Say the sounds in and out of order.*

| at | hen<br>head | in | on | up | day | see<br>happy<br>he | high<br>find | blow<br>no |
|---|---|---|---|---|---|---|---|---|
| zoo | look | car | for<br>door<br>snore | fair | whirl | shout | boy<br>spoil |

*Each box contains one sound but sometimes more than one grapheme. Focus graphemes are **circled**.*

# Green words

f<u>air</u>   p<u>oor</u>   f<u>or</u>   m<u>ore</u>   kn <u>ow</u>   d<u>ar</u>k

f<u>ir</u>   f<u>ir</u>st   th <u>ir</u>d   st<u>ir</u>   b<u>ir</u>d   d<u>ir</u>t   s<u>ir</u>   ch <u>ir</u>p   squ <u>ir</u>m   squ <u>ir</u>t

---

*Read in syllables.*

al`w<u>ays</u>   →   alw<u>ays</u>       im`p<u>or</u>`tant   →   imp<u>or</u>tant

thir`ty   →   th<u>ir</u>ty       el`e`p<u>h</u>ant   →   elep<u>h</u>ant

con`f<u>ir</u>m   →   conf<u>ir</u>m

---

*Read the root word first and then with the ending.*

<u>wh</u> <u>ir</u>l   →   <u>wh</u> <u>ir</u>led       admit   →   admi<u>tt</u>ed

tw<u>ir</u>l   →   tw<u>ir</u>led

f<u>ir</u>m   →   f<u>ir</u>mly

<u>th</u> <u>ir</u>st   →   <u>th</u> <u>ir</u>sty

## Red words

would   want   th<u>eir</u>   wa<u>tch</u>   som<u>e</u>   <u>there</u>   s<u>ai</u>d
a<u>ll</u>   wat<u>er</u>

## Challenge words

f<u>eathers</u>   front

# King of the birds

### Introduction

*Who would you choose to be in charge of your school –*
*someone who looked good or someone who was honest and*
*kind? What is the most important thing about a leader?*
*The birds decide they need a new leader because they are*
*always quarrelling. Crow wants to be the leader but he*
*thinks no one will choose him because he doesn't have*
*beautiful feathers. But do you think that is important? It*
*is not beautiful feathers that will make a good King of the*
*Birds; it is something much more important.*

*What do you think it will be?*

Story written by Gill Munton
Illustrated by Tim Archbold

# Vocabulary check

Discuss the meaning (as used in the story) after the children have read each word.

| | definition: | sentence/phrase: |
|---|---|---|
| **grand** | *important* | *A grand king of all the birds.* |
| **dull** | *boring, plain* | *I look too dull to be king.* |
| **no chance** | *no way of being chosen* | *As for me - I've got no chance.* |
| **display** | *show off* | *Cockatoo was the first to display himself.* |
| **pranced** | *walked proudly* | *As he pranced in front of the birds...* |

*Punctuation to note in this story:*
*1. Capital letters to start sentences and full stops to end sentences*
*2. Capital letters for names*
*3. Exclamation marks to show anger, shock and surprise*
*4. Apostrophe to show contraction: can't  you're*

# King of the birds

Parrot and Jay were sitting in the branches of a dark fir tree.

They were having a quarrel.

"We birds are always quarrelling," chirped Parrot.

"What we need is a king. A grand king of all the birds, to see that we play fair."

Jay agreed.

They set a day for all the birds to have an important meeting.

At the meeting, they would choose a king.

Poor Crow was upset.

"No one will choose me," he chirped sadly.

"I look too dull to be a king.

Cockatoo looks fantastic!

And look at little Hummingbird!

As for me – I've got no chance."

All the birds wanted to be picked to be king, so they went to the Elephant Pond for a wash and brush-up.

Thirsty elephants, drinking at the pond, squirted the birds' feathers with water, and crocs brushed the dirt off with their teeth.

Crow was watching all this.

He spotted some bright feathers – red, gold and green –
that Cockatoo and Hummingbird had dropped on the grass.

When the rest of the birds had whirled off to the meeting,
he picked up the feathers and stuck them on to his back with mud.

"What a handsome bird!"
he chirped to himself.

Thirty birds, big and small, sat in the fir tree. The meeting began.

Cockatoo was the first to display himself.
The rest agreed that he was indeed a most splendid bird.

The second was little Hummingbird.
He twirled amidst the branches,
his bright feathers whirring
and flashing.

The third bird was Crow.
As he pranced in front of the watching birds,
a red feather fell off his back and drifted on to the grass.

There was a stir in the branches of the fir tree,
and the rest of the birds began an angry chirping.

"You have tricked us, sir!" said Cockatoo firmly.
"You may have a handful of bright feathers,
but we can see that you are still just dull old Crow."

Crow squirmed, and three more feathers fell off.

"You're right, Cockatoo," he chirped, looking at his feet.
"I was silly to pretend. I know it was wrong.

I may still be dull old Crow -
but that's not so bad, you know.
We can't all be as splendid as you.
Maybe a dull old Crow would be a good king."

Cockatoo nodded slowly, and so did Hummingbird,
and Jay, and then Parrot.

"You're right, Crow," said Parrot at last.
"You have admitted that you did wrong,
and that shows that you are a good bird.
That's more important than what you look like.
I think you'd be a terrific king."

And he was.

# Questions to talk about

*Re-read the page. Read the question to the children. Tell them whether it is a* **FIND IT** *question or* **PROVE IT** *question.*

**FIND IT**

✓ *Turn to the page*

✓ *Read the question*

✓ *Find the answer*

**PROVE IT**

✓ *Turn to the page*

✓ *Read the question*

✓ *Find your evidence*

✓ *Explain why*

| | | |
|---|---|---|
| **Page 9:** | PROVE IT | *Why did Parrot and Jay decide they needed a king?* |
| **Page 10:** | FIND IT | *Why did Crow think no one would pick him to be the king?* |
| **Page 11:** | FIND IT | *Why did all the birds go to the Elephant Pond?* |
| **Page 12:** | PROVE IT | *What was Crow's plan?* |
| **Page 13:** | FIND IT | *How did Cockatoo and Hummingbird try to impress the other birds?* |
| **Page 14:** | PROVE IT | *How did the other birds feel about Crow's plan?* |
| **Page 15:** | PROVE IT | *What made the other birds choose Crow in the end? Were they right? Who would you choose?* |

# Questions to read and answer

*(Children complete without your help.)*

1. Why does Parrot think they need a king?

2. Why did the birds go to the Elephant Pond?

3. Why did Crow pick up the feathers?

4. What did Crow do with the feathers?

5. Why was Crow the king?

# Speed words

*Children practise reading the words across the rows, down the columns and in and out of order clearly and quickly.*

| wrong | slowly | little | important | for |
|---|---|---|---|---|
| agreed | third | thirty | birds | firm |
| thirsty | first | could | would | you |
| some | kind | old | all | does |